How to Become A Model Christian

(15Attributes of a Model Christian)

Abridged Version

DILLON ST.E BURGIN

Published by Harmony Tabernacle
www.pastorburgin.com
www.harmonytabernacle.org

Copyright ©2016 by Dillon St. E. Burgin

All rights reserved. No part of this publication may be produced, stored in a retrieval system, or transmitted in any form or by any means, electronic, mechanical, Photocopying, recording or otherwise, without the prior permission of the copyright owner.

Published 2016 in corporation with
Dillon St. E Burgin; Brooklyn, NY

Unless otherwise indicated, scripture quotations in this publication are from the Holy Bible, New International Version ©1973, 1978, 1984, International Bible Society.

Dedication

This book is dedicated to my wife Carlene

Carlene Sampson-Burgin is by far the most virtuous woman I've known. She has a quiet strength that is well blended with a genuine love for the Lord. She is a fruitful vine that is watered by a deep sense of humility. I owe her so much. When I began my relationship with her over two decades ago I fondly called her Angel. She has worn that name like a snugly fitted dress; and she has worn it with such dignity that I could not imagine a more fitting helpmeet for me and a better queen to mother, bear and nurture our sons Daniel and Diallo.

Acknowledgement

I thank God for giving me the privilege to have undergone the journey that resulted in this tool for the making of model Christians. He could have used anyone else. But he chose me, and I am grateful.

Thanks to my precious and virtuous wife Carlene who stood by me with much encouragement and prayer while I wrestled with the Lord in an isolated room for days. She did a marvelous job in withholding my lively sons from disturbing my journey.

Thanks to Theresa Jeremiah who graciously undertook the task of edition the original text and made this abridged version possible. Finally, I thank my ecclesiastical flock for their participation in the studies which were born out of the sermons and notes that I presented to them over a period of months.

CONTENTS

Foreword ……………………….............7

Introduction ...………………………......10

1. Attribute #1 - Forgiven & Forgive …..12
2. Attribute #2 - Save all you Can ……...19
3. Attribute #3 - Give your Best   ……….23
4. Attribute # 4 - Repay & Return ……...29
5. Attribute # 5 - Respect ……………….35
6. Attribute # 6 - Prayer………………...41
7. Attribute #7 - Personal substance …..46
8. Attribute #8 - Time ………………….53
9. Attribute # 9 - Multiply Resources …58
10. Attribute #10 - Work …………….....68
11. Attribute #11 - Recreation …………75
12. Attribute #12 - Love Yourself ……...81
13. Attribute #13 - Love others ………...86
14. Attribute #14 - Know who you are…92
15. Attribute #15 - Sold out ……………101

Foreword

This booklet is the product of a series of sermons and bible studies that I conducted over a two year period. The attributes that are herein discussed were given to me during an intense period of fasting and prayer. I received them while I was in deep meditation around the clock for several days seeking a word from the Lord, and pleading with the Lord to relieve me of the deep darkness and misery that had come over me. Everything I put my hands to failed. People I depended on and trusted turned their backs on me. I was in such deep financial trouble that I lost my business and I could not even pay my rent.

In the midst of such deep darkness I ran to the Lord pleaded with Him for relief and for answers. He answered me. And from his answer, I came away with the model for my new Church, the structure of its ministries, the fifteen points of doctrine for its stability and a series of sermons which bore the name of this book. I am deeply grateful to God for the journey which gave birth to these wonderful things, though if I must be perfectly honest, I really did not appreciate the factors that led up to my undertaking the journey.

But isn't it true that the believer will often not give himself as fully as he should, or listen to the Lord as he should, or to do what the Lord requires unless he is struck down and is made to look into the wonderful face of God because he has nowhere else to look?

You can be a model Christian! You shall be a model Christian!!

These attributes are not in order of importance, for they are all important in a linear or cyclical way. However, I will suggest that the order in which they appear gives some sense of progression. That is to say, their order is a good indication of how one can progress more smoothly once the previous stage is engaged and applied. An important caveat here is that all of the attributes have to be done simultaneously because each one helps the other. In fact the believer will find himself/herself stationed at different stages at the same time; working on more than one attribute at a time.

Dillon St. E Burgin

Introduction

Attributes are good, strong, outstanding, indelible, important qualities.

There are Christians and there are model Christians. Just like the U.S army advertisement says 'There is strong and there is army strong"

The apostle Paul talks about the importance of the qualities with which we ought to occupy our minds. He said in Philippians 4:8 "whatsoever things are noble, right, lovely, just and pure; think on these things."

The goal of this study is to lead you to the serendipity of what God desires to give to you and to do in and through you. We all need to live with a sense of purpose. However, God is looking for believers who will develop a sense of purpose about his ultimate purpose of redeeming the world to himself.

Anything that is going to be used and kept as a model must be developed. This is good news in that it encourages us to keep making the effort to grow in our walk with God. In other words, we are encouraged to not let ourselves become frustrated by process and the period over which we evolve into model Christians.

A model Christian is a rosy Christian….
- Like a rose which can be identified from a distance,
- Like a rose that is an enduring symbol of pure love and intimacy,
- Like a rose that has its attached thorns that warns of its preciousness and the need to respect its beauty,
- Like a rose that has an appreciable though not intolerable fragrance……

So is the believer who becomes a model Christian

Attribute #1
Forgiven & Forgive

A model Christian is forgiven and forgives.

Forgiveness is important for everyone because it is the better of two choices. The first of these two choices is unforgiveness. When you do not forgive someone, you automatically choose to hold on to hurts and to risk becoming bitter. Even when you are not aware of it, unforgiveness lurk in your subconscious mind waiting for the most inopportune moment to raise its ugly head. I remember receiving a call one day. It seemed as if that call came out of nowhere. It came one afternoon while I was getting ready to go to pick up my children from school. The caller identified himself. He was rather cordial in his manner and tone of voice. As soon as I realized who he was, my antennas went up. I felt uncomfortable. I was guarded in my responses to his questions. In other words, my guards were up and my sword was out. Let me say it to you in an honest down to earth manner – I was upset that the person actually called me. You see, he had done me some wrong in the past. I had asked the Lord on several occasions to help me to forgive him and to let it go. I thought I did. Then when I received the call I realized that I did not fully let it go. I had to repent. I felt upset with myself that I had not let go of the hurt as much as I thought I did.

The other choice is forgive the other person and to truly let go of that person from your heart. When we forgive others, we give ourselves the gift of freedom to move ahead. In Galatians 6:7 the apostle Paul said, "Do not be deceived. God is not mock. What you sow, you also reap". This text can be applied in a number of ways. But let us apply it to our thoughts on forgiveness. When we forgive other, we open ourselves for God's forgiveness. Isn't that what we mean when we say in the Lord's Prayer "forgive is our debts (or our trespasses) as we forgive our debtors (or those who trespass against us). The other side to this issue of reaping is that when we sow un-forgiveness, we reap bitterness from within ourselves, and additionally, we reap the negative energy that comes from the un-forgiveness of others whom we may have wronged. It is important to realize that even with the best of intention; every one of us wrongs someone at some point in our lives. Therefore, when we forgive others we sow the seed of forgiveness so that we may reap its fruits when our turn to be forgiven comes.

In Matthew 18:21-25 we read the story of the men who owed a king. One could not pay, so he asked for mercy. The king forgave him. But then he went out and punished his fellow worker who owed him - even though the fellow worker begged him for mercy. In telling the story, Jesus said that the king was so upset when he heard what the forgiven man did, so much so, that the King had the man severely punished.

What we learn from that story is that God gets quite upset with us when we refuse to forgive, no matter how hard it is to let go of the wrong that the other person committed against us.

I once heard of a woman who was very sick for a few years. She became too sick to leave home. Her pastor regularly visited her over the years of her illness.

One day he acted out of discernment by asking her if she was holding on to some hurt and un-forgiveness. She admitted that she was holding on to some deep un-forgiveness which had made her bitter because of the person whom she least expected to have hurt her so badly. The pastor led the woman into a mental and spiritual exercise to help her to let go of the unforgiveness. She did. And miraculously, she got well enough to return to Church the following week.

Many people experience what is called Psycho-somatic illness. It is physical sickness that results from mental anguish, guilt, and anger. Thankfully, we can become free of such illness when we forgive.

When you realize that you are forgiven, you will be motivated to forgive. And when you forgive, you experience freedom.

The model Christian lives in his/her forgiveness. When you have un-forgiveness in your heart, it is like acid. It will eat away at your inner self. In 1corinthinan 6:20 Paul says "you were bought with a price, so glorify Christ with your body". This means that when we allow our bodies to go through the trauma and guilt that comes from un-forgiveness, our inner state disallows our bodied from glorifying God. When we accept the forgiveness of God, we are ready for some new and meaningful relationships.

If a man refuses to forgive his mother for something wrong she has done to him, he will not be able to truly love his wife. Similarly, the woman who has not forgiven her father for something he has done to her will not be able to truly love and serve her husband.

My grandmother was an excellent example of the power of forgiveness. My grandfather was unfaithful to her for years. But she stayed in the relationship and when he became too old and too sick to live his usual life, she became his spiritual leader. While he was in his bed of sickness she regularly prayed with him and she assigned their grand children to read the scriptures to him daily.

Forgiveness can confuse the people who we forgive, either because they do not expect it or because they know that they do not deserve it. However, you must never forgive a person only to show yourself as the bigger person or to be arrogant. Forgiveness relieves you of hurt, anger, envy, malice and bitterness. It also requires a right spirit and a humble attitude to enable it to have its full effect.

Answer the following Questions
1. Is there anyone in your life whom you have not forgiven?
2. Is there anyone in your life whom you need to ask for forgiveness?

Do the following exercises:
1. Make time today (don't let a week pass) to reach out to that person. If the situation is too tense and wisdom dictates that now is not the time to do it, then do the next exercise.
2. Pray every day for the next seven days for any specific individual who has wronged you or whom you need to forgive. Ask God to release you and to release that person from the weight of un-forgiveness.

Attribute #2
Save all you can

A Model Christian saves all he/she can.

This principle on the surface refers to money. However, it is a larger principle than money.
It means that we should not be wasteful. And we should plan for the future.
Sometimes people are not able to save a lot of money or any money for that matter, because of circumstances in their life. Nevertheless, we should work towards being able to do so. This matter will come up later on in our journey through these attributes. Let us look at the deeper levels of what it means to say that becoming a model Christian save all he can. Here is the interpretation of that attribute: - Respect time, respect your money, respect your relationship, and respect your health.

Do not waste time or money. And do not abuse your relationships. Moreover, take care of your body by exercising and eating healthy. Here is a nugget for my male readers - One of the fastest ways to become poor is to become a womanizer. To the rest of you, one of the fastest ways to reduce your assets is to become itinerant (i.e. to change your address too often even when it is for the sake of a job).

When you save it is a sign that you are planning ahead because you know the value of the seed you have. It also shows that you have some vision of what the Lord has in store for you.

There is a saying that goes this way - "willful waste brings woeful want." Sometimes it is rendered "waste not/want not". You get the idea. If we waste what we are blessed with, then we will reap a lack of what we really need.

In the gospel of Luke 15:11-32 we find the story of a rich and sometimes wasteful family. The prodigal younger brother found out that pig's food looks really attractive when you are really hungry. He had wasted what he received from his father's estate. Had he respected the money he started out with, the relationship the father had cultivated with his family over the years, and the energy it took to build up the resources in the family, his story may have been much more transformational. He had learnt some valuable lessons through his wasteful or prodigal choices. I guess you could say the wisdom found in Proverbs 6:26 come alive in his life that "A man who spends time with prostitute will become bread."

Answer the following Questions
1. Have you ever been wasteful with your time, your money or your talent?
2. Have you changed or adjusted your behavior over the last seven months?

3. Have you calculated what your wasteful behavior has cost you?

Do the following exercises:
1. Calculate the potential value of your time if you were to make better use of it. In other word, calculate how much more influence, knowledge and projects you would have achieved if you commit less time to some of your current activities; and if you commit more of your time to other activities.

2. Do the exercise above, relating it to your ***Time.***

3. Do the same exercise above, relating it to your ***Talent.***

Remember - The key here is to examine what you have been doing with your ***time, talent, skills and money.*** Then do a projection and calculation of what you could and should be doing with those gifts.

Attribute #3
Give your Best

A model Christian gives of his/her best.

It is not necessarily a noble thing to give away things to people, merely because you do not want them anymore. Sometimes, people will give away things that they own, only because they have already bought a replacement.

It is a good stretch of your will and your spirit to get something new for someone on the grounds that you are convinced of this one thing - it's good enough for the other person because it's good enough for you.

I have developed the habit of giving the best of what I do for my family. For example, if I prepare two sandwiches for myself and one of my children or my wife asks me for a sandwich, I deliberately give the better one to the person who asks.

In Philippians 2:3 we find this principle - "Do nothing from selfish ambition or conceit. But in humility regard others as better than yourself." We need to frequently assume this posture of humility mixed with an appreciation for the value of other people. You will find that as you do this, your inner happiness increases and your love for others multiply.

Romans 12:3 states "For by the grace given to me I say to you, not to think of yourself more highly than you ought to..." This scripture reinforces the value of the Christian secret, that when we look at ourselves through the lens of the grace or the favor of God, we operate with a sense of gratitude. This gratitude comes from the awareness that God could have chosen someone else to have the privilege of serving in your capacity, yet God chose you. As long as our focus is on the God who gives us the opportunity, we can humble ourselves to appreciate the chance to serve.

Now comes the sweet part - Galatians 6:7 "What you sow you reap." In this principle we are given the expectation that we will be served to the extent that we serve, and to the degree of joy with which we serve others. What this means is that we can expect others to serve us without thinking that we are beneath them as opposed to thinking that we do deserve to be served by them. Moreover, when they give us their best, they do so with a light and glad heart because they know that we deserve it In return.

Let me recommend that you do the following as a good exercise to help you develop your ability to give of your best: - repeat these words to yourself "I sow the best. I will reap the best. I shall reap the best. I must reap the best."

In Mark 8:36 Jesus asked "What shall it profit a man if he should gain the whole world, but lose his own soul". The point here is it does not make sense if you have all the material things in the world, but you live without peace. If you become wealthy and prosperous but it is only "for me", then you have not done well. You can say that you have done well only when you pull up others as you move up.

The gospel of Luke 6:38 makes this bold promise from God "Give and it will be given to you, good measure, pressed down, shaken together and running over, will the Lord give onto you".

We ought to give out of a sense of duty to God. Also, we ought to have joy in giving. Sometimes it will be inconvenient to give; yet even in those times, we must give. In the case of money, you can only defy the power of money by giving it away. This is also why the principle of tithing is so important. In tithing, we say to God, 'the first of what I have is yours, and the rest of what I keep will be used to glorify you through me.'

In the end, this principle impresses upon you the need to invest in the kingdom of God.

You do so by giving your best to others, planning for the future, and making room in your life for the blessings of God to multiply.

Answer the following Questions
1. Do you do most of your activities for your own benefits or for the benefits of others?
2. Do you ever give of your best and then talk about it afterwards?

Do the following exercises:
1. Examine your motive for doing everything that you do in life. Then try to figure out how you might be able to create a good or better balance between what you do for your own sake and what you do merely for the good of others. *[**Truth be told, we do not do anything purely for other. Everything we do for others has at least a tiny bit of self-interest - even if it is merely the feeling of being a good person or a model Christian].*

2. Do some special things for three people in your life this week, knowing that you will not benefit from what you do for them. Make sure that these people really need your help even if it will cause you some inconvenience.

Attribute # 4
Repay & Return

A model Christian repays and returns what he/she borrows.

Let me start this section on a personal note of confession. I have actually borrowed things and not return them. As a high school boy, I borrowed a book on first Aid from one of my friends. I found the book years later, and I really felt that I should have returned it. However, I did not know where to find my classmate. So I held on to the book.

As an adult, I borrowed money from my friends to save my business when I was in a particularly difficult situation. I could not pay back all the money because my plans did not work out the way I expected. Needless to say, I lost a couple of "friends."

If I am ever asked to give my candid advice on borrowing money, I will say the following:

- unless you are in a dire life and death situation, never borrow money from a "friend." Worse yet, never borrow money from a "stranger." Since you have observed that I enclosed the words "friend" and "stranger" with quotation marks, let me explain why.

The best friends you will have are the people who have known you from the earlier years of your life or the people who have had the chance to journey beside you in some particularly difficult situation. I have found that the friends who have come to know you over the course of a few years really do not know your story well enough to accurately judge your heart and your motive.

"Stranger" is the person who has recently come to know you. Generally, that person may have met you in your professional capacity, or at a fraternal gathering or in a business conference. These people really do not know you. Therefore, if you were to borrow anything from them, let alone money, they see you largely in your professional capacity, not a real friend. This obviously makes for an unhealthy situation if you cannot repay them.

When you borrow anything from anyone, you actually receive trust from them. If you borrow from an unbeliever and cannot repay what you borrowed, some of them would be too happy to blame "Christians" for being untrustworthy or may call them fakes.

The principle of repaying means that you are able to honor your word. At the heart of repaying what you borrow, is the notion of honoring the trust that the lender placed in you, and honoring the commitment that you made to them.

Try to fulfill your promise and the expectation that you give people. It is on the borrower to not let down himself/herself or the other person.

In 1 peter 3:9 we read "Do not repay evil with evil or insult with insult, but with a blessing in order that you may receive a blessing". So God wants us to repay evil with good and repay good with good.

Psalm 37:21 states "The wicked borrow and do not repay but the righteous gives generously". The point here is that the wicked will look for opportunity to cheat and deceive, but the righteous look for opportunity to bless and to repay.

If you are a believer, you ought to work towards the time when you can cut up all of your credit cards, burn your mortgage; and burn your car note etc. This will put you in a position to say, "Had it not been for God on my side, where would I be".

One implication of this principle is that groups of believers must come together to help each other to get to this place of self-sufficiency. Working together can help each other to grow as individuals and consequentially, the group itself will grow.

We must see the importance of developing a common vision. We must also build projects and programs together. When we learn to do this as we see in the book of Acts, the shared burden will become lighter and the shared blessing will multiply.

We need to borrow some trust, some confidence, some love, and some kindness. Also, we must lend some of these same qualities. When we can do all of this, we will find that our lives become easier and more enjoyable.

Answer the following Questions

1. What do you think the bible actually means when it says in Psalm 22:7 "The wicked borrow and do not repay"?
2. How do you explain this verse from the bible – Romans 13:8 "Owe no one anything except to love each other."?

Do the following exercises:

1. Sketch out a plan for how you will repay the people you owe - whether you owe them money or other

material possessions. You may need to seek professional help if the matter has legal requirement and restrictions that you will need to meet.

2. Draft out a detail plan of what you will do to ensure that you generate enough money and assets to prevent you from becoming a repeat borrower over the course of your life.

Attribute # 5
Respect

A model Christian respects his/her parents, children and siblings.

When I became a preacher, one of the things I did was to write a letter to my father who was living in another country. I also wrote a letter to my mother in which I said to her "I am not the boy that you did not get a chance to raise, but I would like to establish a healthy adult relationship with you."

In both cases it worked out well. My dad was the proudest papa in town when I invited him to my wedding and he flew in for it. Today, my mum refers to me often as Reverent or Pastor. She still sends me daily inspirational messages via social media; and we speak to each other often via telephone. In Romans 13:7 we are instructed to "give to everyone what you owe him…… Revenue…. Respect… Honor…"

Goodwill and respect is due to everyone. Moreover, we can actually change people's lives because we communicate to them that they are worthy indeed of our attention and they have a rightful place in society. Romans 12:10 commands us to "be devoted to one another in brotherly love."

We can actually learn to have and to show affection to other people even when we do not really know them. When we develop this kind of affection or brotherly love towards them, we fulfill a requirement from God. At the same time, we make ourselves more beautiful and we put pressure on others to be more beautiful also.

In Ephesians 6:1-2 Paul commands children to "obey your parents in the Lord…." You should not expect things to go well with you if you treat your parents with disrespect and meanness. If you treat your siblings or parents badly, you will reap evil. Exodus 20:12 "Honor your father and mother." This is not a suggestion, it is a command.

The Old Testament concept of Honor actually means that you give the person some authority in your life. Hence, to honor one's parents means that you should pay attention to their wisdom and insight because this makes them feel important. It also lets us into their reservoir of experience and insight.

One of the most important ways in which we can respect the people in our lives is by carefully choosing our words.

The Bible says that the tongue is a dangerous weapon. We have all witnessed some situation in which things got out of hand because the wrong words were exchanged and were intensified. Many marriages ended because of the tongue. In fact, women are by far more capable than men in destroying lives with their mouth. It is their most lethal weapon.

We have heard it said "Stick and stone may break my bone, but words can't hurt me." This is false in every way. For this reason God's word says in Proverbs 15:1 "Soft words turn away rage but grievous words stir up anger." Again the word says that "the power of life and death are in the tongue." Proverbs 18:21.
How can one be a real believer if she plays music in church, sings in the choir, gives tithe and offering etc., but she does not relate to her siblings or parents? This will not work well. In fact her own children may develop unhealthy rivalry and discord, because she may have sown the seed of discord with her own siblings or relatives." You ought not to feel that you are alright until the other person is alright.

Answer the following Questions
1. 1Peter 3:9 states, "do not repay evil for evil or insult with insult."
2. Do you believe that there are times when you have to say or do something harsh in order to correct a situation or to get across your point?
3. How is your relationship with your spouse, your siblings and your children? Rate your relationship and your level of interaction with these relatives on a scale of 1 to 10 in which ten represents the highest and healthiest relationship.

Do the following exercises:
1. Make a list of the main issues or actions that resulted in a damaged relationship with your spouse, your sibling or your children. If your relationship with your family members is good or great, make a list of the things that make it so.

Use the space below to do this now:

_____
_____
_____

2. Make a list of the **main** issues or the actions that can improve the respect between you and your spouse, sibling and children:

_____
_____

Over the next week, begin to practice the things you listed above.

Attribute # 6
Pray

A model Christian prays often for self and others.

1 Thessalonians 5:17 commands the believer to "Pray without ceasing" or "pray continually"
In Ephesians 5:19 the believer is encouraged to "Speak to one another with psalms, hymns and spiritual songs…" This makes me think of Mr. Graham who stops by our office often just to say hello to my wife and I. He always has a word or a passage of scripture which we would discuss, not as a study, but as healthy conversation. We do such a good job at encouraging each other through this simple Christian interaction.

    By contrast to that story, I have observed over the years of my ministry that I do not enjoy calling or being called on the phone by some of my pastor colleagues. Often, they are more interested in talking about the other pastors who have been transferred or who are having problems at their church. They are more interested in basking in or in merely reporting the misfortunes and challenges of other pastors, instead of discussing the things of God that are edifying. In fact, if they would suggest that in the conversation we should pause and pray for the others that would be so much more helpful. It would also put a smile on God's face.

When you pray for people, it gives you a different attitude towards them. Sometimes, when you pray for people, you may discover that you are actually the problem. You may discover that you have been judgmental or that your attitude has not been great. Remember that you must talk with God about others before you talk with them about God.

Concerning your own self - when you pray, you must be specific in your prayers. Do not merely say "O Lord bless me!" Rather, you should ask the Lord to give you a break through. Ask God to show you specific people and place where you can be blessed.

Part of being focused and specific in our prayers to God is that we must seek God on God's terms. When you seek God on your own terms, you will find yourself in the proverbial desert for forty years. This is the essence of what the Hebrews did while they were in the wilderness. Sometimes, God is giving us an idea, or a vision or a strategy; but we are too busy trying to let God see our way, thus we end up confused and frustrated.

God's power is at work in our lives. This means that God want to perfect and to favor us. God knows our hearts and our intentions. We must ask God to make our intentions good and righteous because God does not only look at our actions. He also looks at our heart. How can we have good relationships with others if we do not honor God our heavenly parent or Jesus our brother? We must ask God to help us to do our best even when it is inconvenient to do so.

Answer the following Questions

1. Are you satisfied with the level of your prayer life and the frequency of your daily prayers?
2. Do you make use of printed prayer or do you only pray from your own thoughts and from your heart?

Do the following exercises:

1. Find a book of prayers and begin to use it at least once every day as a tool to talk to God in a structured way. After one week, write out your own prayer and start to say it regularly. Let this inspire you to talk with God intelligently on a regular basis.

2. Starting this week, look for models of prayer in the Bible and begin to pray like the people who made those prayers to God. One good place to begin is in the psalms. *[You will find that there are prayers for deliverance, prayers against your enemies, prayers for your own deliverance, prayers for success and wealth and so on]*.

Attribute #7
Personal substance
A model Christian honors God with his/her personal substance.

Your personal substance means your sex life, your relationship, your inner life, your desires, and your habits.
When everything else is stripped away, God wants **YOU**. This attribute is dealing with you in a very personal way.

Honor God with your sex life
The Greek word 'porneia' is the one that is commonly used in the bible to refer to sexual impropriety. It is from the same word we get the word pornography. The word is used to warn us against any form of sexual behavior and attitudes that are bent solely on satisfying the flesh or our physical pleasures.

This is the reason why Paul says in 1 Corinthians 6:18-20 "Shun fornication ……. Every sin is outside the body…but fornication is against the body…you were bought with a price; therefore glorify God with your body…."

The reason prostitutes and men who run around are so unhappy is that through sexual intercourse, the individual is actually and literally sharing himself/herself with the other person. Therefore, the more sexual partners the individual has means that that person is shared up into that many parts. This dishonors God and it defaces the image of God in the individual.

Honor God in the area of your relationship

In 2 Corinthians 6:14 we are given a warning - "Do not be mismatched with unbelievers…" I think back to the time when I met the lady who would become my wife. I was delighted to hear her say that she had committed herself to "not marry a divorcee or an unbeliever." I think you can guess why this was good news to my ear - I was neither of those two things. I was single, never been married, and saved.

This principle of not being unequally yoked is also important for business. For example, I personally know a woman who trusted an acquaintance by giving him a share in her business. After a short time of having the man in the business, the woman was pushed out and the man took away the business from her.

In the King James Version of the Bible the word is

"Be not unequally yoked…" The image here is that of two Cattles joined together by the head and shoulder with a wooden contraption that keeps them together while they pull along a cart or a plow. The implication of this image is that if you do not share a sameness of purpose, values and vision with the other person, you may run into serious problems and end up with regrets

Honor God with your inner Life

Romans 12:2 cautions us "Do not be conformed to this world but be transformed by the renewing of your mind…." The point here is that you must focus fully on God with your inner life. If you do so, the world will not be able to force you to easily adjust to its ways; which usually contradicts that which God requires of you.

Honor God with your desires

In James1:12-16 we find this encouragement - "Blessed is anyone who endures temptation…. Everyone is drawn away by their own desires…" Our desires lure, entice and entrap us. The fulfillment of ungodly desires always leads to and involves sinful experiences. This snow ball of sin leads to destruction (death). When we get wrapped up in sinful activities, we lose a part of ourselves. In other word, something dies within us.

We must try hard not to lose our spiritual innocence. Whenever that happens, it opens the door to every other kind of sin and destruction. That is why the Bible says, "Sin, when it is grown brings forth death." When you engage in sin, after a while you become immune to the guilty feeling accompany sin. For this reason, you must never let your heart become callous and seared that you are no longer sensitive to God or you are no longer sensitive to the blight of sin.

Honor God with your habits

There is an old rhyme about HABIT. It says that when you take the "H" off of habit, you still have "abit." When you take "A" off, you still have "bit". And when you take away the "B" you still have "it".

Paul cautions against the very course of action that could lead to some bad and destructive habits. He says in I Corinthians 6:12 "All things are lawful for me, but I will not get engage in everything."

Sometimes people take a liberal approach to life. They say that one should not be too stiff and proper; that that one should "enjoy life". What happens to such people is that they develop habits which they are neither happy about nor proud of. In fact these kinds of habits become prisons for the person who has them.

Answer the following Questions
1. Do you give at least 10 percent of your time and your skills and your money to the service of God through a God-honoring ministry?
2. Are you faithful to your spouse or to your fiancé? Are you faithful to the Lord in your personal behavior and attitudes; or have you developed a few bad habits which have been

getting in the way between you and the Lord?

Do the Following Exercises:

1. If you have been dating for a while, go to a marriage advisor, a counselor or a qualified Pastor and make preparations to marry the person. If in your judgment this relationship is not compatible, end it sooner rather than later.
2. Begin to spend at least three minutes every day in silence (this means without music, computer, radio etc.) listening to God and taking note of how God can get closer to you. Ask God to show you how to use every area of your personal life to make him satisfied with you.

Attribute #8
Time

A model Christian uses his/her time for the glory of God.

This attribute means that you ought to use your time wisely and sparingly.
The psalmist acknowledged in Psalm 31:15 "My times are in your hand." We often say "I don't have time." This is quite an accurate statement. God is the one who has time. God lends us His time. Therefore, we can make the best use of our time when we surrender our every moment to God so that He can fully direct our use of every minute we are given.
In Psalm 90:12 we find this humble request, "teach us to number our days so we may apply our hearts to wisdom." I have witnessed the beauty of a person who lived a full and satisfied life, and then she

assumed a waiting position for God. This woman had lived well and had much satisfaction. So she was ready to go home to the Lord in peace.

There is something to this idea of "numbering your days." In other words, the believer ought to prayerfully look ahead and make plans for the legacy he wishes to leave in the wake of his death.
Ecclesiastes 3:1-8 tells us "There is a time for everything…" This is a statement of fact. It is not permission for you to do whatever you wish. It is a challenge for you to know what season you are in and how to get the best out of your season.
Paul puts it this way in Ephesians 5:15-16 "Be careful how you live….making the most of the time".

The point here is that the believer must never become satisfied with simply having flexible time. In fact I would argue that the believer never has such a thing as "spare time." All time is God's time.

Therefore, we must spend every moment living our lives fully by working to improve our own lives, the lives of others, and even the planet. The implication here is, even when we do not have to go somewhere specific, nor do we have a set task, we must still not look at our time as "spare time." Instead we must at least spend the time praying and meditating.

Sometimes, we can just decide to relax or take a vacation. But even then we must understand these activities as part of what it means to be occupied in renewing the body and the mind.

The great evangelist John Wesley cautioned his readers to not spend more time than is necessary in any place.

We ought not live in, or merely nurture the regret that we did not let go or move on earlier than we did. To do so would be wasting our time and wasting precious energy. Instead, we must learn our lessons and become wise about timing. We will figure out how to let go even when we want to hold on for a longer time.

We may need to let go of certain investments, certain relationships and certain traditions. Wise use of our time will dictate that we look carefully at what the thing is doing to us. From this view point, we can then open our minds and our spirits to God, and let Him show us which move to make. Once we do that, we can then confidently decide whether it is time to let go or to hold on.

Answer the following Questions
1. What do you spend most of each day doing? (be specific)
2. How much of your time would you say you waste each day of any given week?

Do the following exercises:
1. Starting today, calculate how much time you spend every week for the next three week talking with your family and planning with your

colleagues/Co-workers/helpers. Use the space provided below:

_____
_____
_____
_____
_____
_____

2. Make a chart or list of the regular activities you do in any given week. Decide which ones are the most important. Give the reason why they are the most important. Allocate more time to the most important activities than to any other ones. Make yourself use the time in the way you laid it out in the chart.

Attribute # 9
Multiply your Resources
(PS+ C+H = MR)

A model Christian learns to multiply his/her resources - PS *(personal substance)* **+ C** *(creativity)* **+H** *(knowledgeable helpers)* **= MR** *(Multiplied Resources).*

This section places a lot of emphasis on these three aspects of a person's development - Time, School and Business. You must learn what to put into your space. In other words learn what to put into the time God has given you. Decide that you are going to learn various skills, learn a trade, get certified or get a degree.

One of the things to bear in mind is that you may well be one of the many people who are called to open and run your own business, but you have been afraid to step out. A bit of encouragement for you here is that only by doing business that you will get a real chance to learn some specialized skills. Moreover, you will learn how systems work, and how to form strategic relationships. The point here is that through the journey of developing yourself, you will become more industrious and you will put your creativity to work like you could have barely imagined.

From the vantage point of long term benefits, when you use your creativity and skills well, what you do in your earlier years will allow you to comfortably retire in your later years. What you put into your younger life will allow you to have less regrets in your later life. What you put into the opportunities you have will allow you to gain greater dividends down the road.

The challenge here is that you must use what you have wisely. The way to do this is to put more into less time, so that you will have more time for other, more creative and enjoyable things.

The Burgin's formula for multiplying your resources is PS+ C+H = MR - Your personal substance plus creativity, plus knowledgeable helpers equal your Multiplied Resources.

John 2:1 and following tells us that Jesus turned water into wine. What this means is that Jesus was showing us that the best way to grow our lives and our value is to turn raw material into other products.

In Matthew 25:14-30 Jesus tells the story of three men who were entrusted with various measures of talents. One of the men made the investor very angry because he buries his in the ground. The implication here is that God Is both saddened and angry when we waste our talents and our opportunities.

One key passage in the bible that challenges us to go beyond using the talent is Ecclesiastes 10:10. It states - "If the axe is dull, much strength is required." This passage is clearly moving us beyond merely having talents and opportunity. It's a passage that pushes us to set the tools and systems in place so that we can prepare ourselves and the resources we have to get more out of our efforts.

If you are not a particularly sharp individual, you may need to make greater effort to achieve your goal. Notwithstanding that point, my interest in this verse at this point is to show you that if we make the preparations and if we set things in place in our lives, we will have a more straight forward path in life. Also, we will be guaranteed less pains. And to a large extent we will have less regrets and losses throughout our life.

Luke 16:1-13 tells the story of the shrewd steward. He ought to raise this question in our minds – 'How can we take what the people of the world have and use it in creative ways?' We need to sanitized the resources of the world and adopt the things which God has shown us so that we can use them for his glory

We have help to do what is suggested above because of this assurance given in Psalm 37:23 "The steps of a good person are ordered by the Lord." This means that we can step out confidently with the right intention, knowing that the Lord will direct us and prosper our ways. It is his desire to do so because he delights in the well-being and the success of His children.

When we use our time wisely and we multiply our resources, God will order our steps and honor us. In fact, it is more accurate to say that God has already ordered our steps. So when we use God's time wisely and we multiply our resources, we will actually find the path that God has already ordered. You see, a highway or a side road does not become existent or accessible because we drive on it. It is already there. However, we discover that it is there when we set our navigation to go in that direction and to use the path or road which has already been provided.

Here is an important set of equations the Lord gave to me:

A). work hard + not work smart = least success

B). Work Smart + not work hard = good Success

C). ***Work smart + work hard = great success***

A word of caution here - Working smart does not in any way imply thievery, trickery, scheming or dishonesty in any shape or form. Rather it categorically refers to the ways in which we can use what we have in ways that are creative, and ways in which we can increase output for the time and energy we put in.

For example, once I was doing some small handyman tasks around the church. I had a sharp hand saw with which I was cutting the board. Then someone came by and said to me, "Pastor, you are wasting your time and making yourself more tired. Why don't you buy a small and inexpensive power saw and do the work?" I checked out the saws at a large hardware and found exactly what I needed. Needless to say, I improved my output and my timing by far.

Answer the following Questions
1. What can you say are definitely your talents? *(Not what you think or what you would like your talent to be).*
2. What skills do you have as a result of formal training, mentoring or schooling?

Do the following exercises:
1. Write this equation in large on an index card and stick it on your mirror: **PS+ C+H = MR.** Every day before you leave home, tell yourself how you will use your time today. Make sure that you think of your time in light of your talent, skills and opportunities.
2. Make a list of the skills you have. Make a list of your monies, material resources, property, work experience,

and the people in your life. Draw a line to connect these resources and decide on how you will lay your role in putting them to work for your own growth and development. Always think of how you can add value to each resource or person – that is the key to the growth and success you seek.

Use the space below to help you:
Monies:

_____
_____
_____

Material resources:

_____
_____
_____

Property:

_____
_____

Work experience:

_____
_____
_____
_____

People in your life:

_____
_____
_____
_____

3. Get hold of a book that will educate you on how you can improve in your area of expertise, so that you can learn how to multiply your efforts. Also, looks up some videos on www.YouTube.com to see how people in your field of expertise are making the greatest success of what you already can do. *[Note - just type in "how to …..(whatever your skill is)]*

4. Write down the following equation in large print on an index card: "***Work smart + work hard = great success".*** Paste the index card on your mirror or carry it in your wallet. Examine yourself to see whether you are working hard and smart or only one of the two. Be honest in this exercise. Now spend some time looking at how you can improve in both areas – smart and hard.

Attribute #10
Work

A model Christian does work that glorifies God.

In 1 Corinthians 10:23-29 we are cautioned that "All things are lawful but not all things are beneficial or build up…." A paraphrase of this scripture may look something like this - 'Not everything you do is good to be done even if you feel like it.' In a more direct statement to the believer, the principle is: you can do anything you want to do as a person. However, the biblical position is, as a believer, you are restricted in what you do since you ought to seek the glory of God above your own pleasurable desires.

    As a believer, you must ask yourself, "Is my work glorifying God?" When I graduated from high school as a young man, I could not find a job. I could have asked my uncle to get me a job as a Bar Tender at the hotel where he worked. However, I was already saved. Hence, I was sure that there were some jobs that I could not do because they would conflict with my Christian values.

　　I actively waited until the Lord opened the door for me. When I say that I actively waited, what I mean is, I spent a lot of my time and energy expanding my small farming business. After two years, the Lord eventually opened the door for me to be gainfully employed as a missionary to rebuild a congregation in the denomination that I grew up in. I now look back on those days as some of the most formative years in my preparation for seminary and for the skills that I have found helpful in ministry over the years.

　　In America today, over seventy-five percent of working people do not enjoy or like the work they do. Whatever you do for a job, you ought to ask the Lord "What is the purpose of this job in my life?" You ought to also ask the Lord "What is my personal purpose in this job, besides working to earn a salary?" It may be that the Lord has put you in that job to help someone become more humble, more respectful, and more appreciative. Nevertheless, you must ask yourself repeatedly, 'Is this what the Lord wants for me?'

Do not simply work in order to feel good about yourself. We are made to work. Hence, we feel useful and worthwhile when we work. Nevertheless, we must seek to be employed in work that generates enough money for us to live on and provide enough for us to save. Whatever you do should multiply you. It should multiply your time, multiply your talent, multiply what you are, and multiply your material possessions.

A model Christian works and creates work. Also, a model Christian seeks work that multiplies him/her. This ambitious and purposeful approach to your work should be motivated by the instruction Paul gives in

Colossians 3:23: "Whatever you do, you ought to do it as if you are really doing it for God". Dr. Martin Luther king put it well, he said that if a person cannot be a tree on the mountain, he must be a shrub in the valley, but be the best shrub there is.

In my own journey, one of my friends at seminary used to call me "Mr. Diligent" because of how I applied myself to study. When I moved to the United States I did some graduate work at Drew University seminary in New Jersey. After graduation, one of my friends said to me that he always admired how I carried myself. He said, "You know you always looked like one of the professors, and I always said to myself, 'This man has the making of a president of this college one day.'" I had a good laugh of appreciation for his esteemed comment and I told him that he was being kind. Needless to say, I took note of what he was really saying at a deeper level. He was saying that I displayed a sense of purpose and a good attitude even while pursuing higher education.

When I was a teenager, I used to help a rich family to do some work around their house. I was not happy doing it. However, I did the work with a smile and I did it with a good attitude. I did the work because I was brought up to respect my elders and to help them out if they ask me to help. Looking back on those years, the old, rich woman whom I helped around the yard blessed me with her words. She also gave me a 'good name.'" She always said "May the Lord bless you. And may the Lord give you a good wife when the time comes for you to marry." I believe that the blessing really served me well because of the wife with which the Lord blessed me.

In Genesis 3:19 we are told that the Lord instructed Adam and eve that they will have to toil and they will have to eat through hard work. Their work became hard after their disobedience. This means that work is intended to be enjoyable and fulfilling. It is intended to enlarge and to enhance who we are. However, sin has turned work into a thing that brings dissatisfaction and stress instead of mere fulfillment.

Therefore, we must deliberately seek work (employment or our own business) that will bring fulfillment and meaning to our lives. Whatever you do for a job must be Profitable morally, financially and spiritually. One key point that is worthy of emphasis here is that even while you are in transition, and you do not like the job that you do, you should still give it your best.

Answer the following Questions

1. Do you believe that what you do for a living glorifies God?
2. Do you like what you do as a job? If not, are you actively looking for something better?

Do the following exercises:

1. Examine your circumstance, your skills and your talent. Make a list of the areas of business you can venture into if you were to be given the opportunity to do your own business or to work as a business partner with someone else.
2. Pray to God for the next seven days, asking God specifically what is your purpose on the earth. Ask Him to reveal to you how the job you are doing now is contributing to that purpose. Then ask Him how your current job is leading you to the next leg of your journey to fulfillment and purpose. Finally, ask Him to lead you to the door that will take you into what your ultimate assignment on the earth is.

Attribute #11
Recreation

A model Christian, you must leave room for recreation.

When most people hear the word recreation, they think of going out with friends, reveling, idling, letting down their hair, drinking and hanging out.

In the context of being a model Christian, we need to look at the word 'recreation' again. Recreation has in it the word "re-create". God wants us to re-create ourselves, our energies, our ideas. God has made the script for our lives. God has deposited within us all that is necessary for our life.

When a vehicle is manufactured, it is supposed to last for a particular period. So if the manufacturer intends the vehicle to last for twenty years, the vehicle has parts that can work well for that period. On the other hand, the vehicle must be serviced periodically. In servicing the vehicle, some parts must be replaced because of wear and tear.

In like manner, God has equipped us with all that we need for the number of years he has already assigned for us to live. However, we will need to do maintenance and upgrades. This is the same as saying, we need to do recreation. In order to become a model Christian, you must become engaged in recreational activities.

Many people die too early because they stop recreating. From my observation, the people who work in jobs where they use their brain a lot, and those who do a lot of research and mentoring, they live longer. Sometimes you meet people who are relatively young but they have the attitude and the disposition of a much older person. Conversely, you sometimes see people who are well up in age, but they are young at heart and their disposition is one of life and vigor.

Recreation is to life what sunshine is to plants. It is for that reason that executives go to a gym or take up a sports pastime. In my own life, I do a combination of jogging and aerobics a few times per week. One of my Pastor friends regularly gets together with some of his male friends to play dominoes. In that circle, he is actually networking and strategizing for his business as well as his ministry while relaxing in that way.

Recreation is not merely reveling, sports or games. Rather, it is engaging in what are authentically you. So do not leave until God tells you to leave. Accept God's instruction and wait for God's timing. Sometimes God shows us things in stages. Being in God's will does not mean that things will be a 'bed of roses' and that everything will work well. Sometimes you are in the center of the will of God having the greatest difficulties you have ever faced. However, God may be leaving you there for a while to learn some lessons both about God and about yourself.

When your work and your recreation become one, that's when you would have found your ministry. Hence the question to you is "Do you have a ministry; or what is your ministry?" What do you feel passionate about? What are you really good at doing while you also enjoy doing it?

If you find something that recreates you while at the same time it is doing well for you financially, morally, and spiritually, then you have found your ministry.

Answer the following Questions

1. What do you do for recreation?
2. How many times per week do you do recreational activities? Is the frequency enough; and if not what is your reason for not doing more?

Do the following exercises:

1. Look again at the equation you wrote on your index card previously: "***Work smart + work hard = great success".*** Now examine

yourself to see whether you are working hard and smart or if you are doing only one side of the equation. Be honest in this exercise. Now spend some time looking at how you can improve in both areas –smart and hard.

2. Get hold of books on health and exercise that will educate you on how you can improve in your physical and mental capabilities. This can greatly help you to train yourself in preserving and multiplying your abilities. It will naturally lead to greater creativity and increased production. When I was a much younger man, I has what you may call a hot temper. My grandmother had a colorful way of describing it. For my part, I knew that a temper can get a person into trouble. I also knew that since I had given my heart to the Lord in my teen years, I should grow in him. And certainly, a temper was did not show growth and godliness. By God's grace, I came across a book, the name of which I do not remember now, although I

think it was one of Norman Vincent peal's books. It had a chapter on how to overcome a temper and anger. I followed the steps and I prayed continuously about it. The method worked. Now people think that I am the most patient and cool person they know.

Another example I would like to share has to do with my love of books. As a youn man I read many pamphlets and story books. As I grew older, I took a real interest in magazines, especially the ones on martial arts. Perhaps I was a product of my the Bruce Lee era, when every boy I knew wanted to become a superstar martial or at least pretended to be one. These magazines taught me some proper techniques on how to exercise safely and how to breathe.

Today, everything is available on the internet through Google and on YouTube. Make full use of these sources. And make sure you follow through on the exercises I suggest in this book. You have a big head start by reading this book. Congratulations.

Attribute #12
Love Yourself

A model Christian loves himself/herself.

A model Christian must be honest in such a way that even when it hurts the other person you will tell them the truth. This is a call for radical love. You should seek to make people respect you even when they do not like you. If people know how big your heart is, they will try to love you even when it is hard.

You must develop love for your own self. In other words you must appreciate yourself even though you may not think that you are the right size or the right shape or that you do not have the right talent.

When I was a teenager, I read the story of a little boy who was teased at school because he was smaller than everyone else. He was always the last to get picked on the team, if he got picked at all. One evening while he was travelling home from school, the school bus on which the boy was travelling feel into a ditch. This rejected boy was the only child who was small enough to climb out through the window of the bus and go to get help. That week the mayor of the city honored the boy for his bravery.

    I once counseled a woman who was having some family problems and some self-esteem issues. At a given moment I suggested a simple exercise she could do in front of her mirror. I told her to stand in front of her mirror every day for a brief moment and simply say to herself "I am beautiful. In God's eyes, I am fearfully and wonderfully made." She quickly informed me that she never looks into the mirror. I was clearly stunned. Needless to say, I immediately realized how deeply wounded and lost that woman was to herself and to her God-given purpose.

One of the other things you must love about yourself is your temperament. Temperament is the combination of a person's mental and emotional traits or their natural predisposition. God has a reason for making you the way you are. For example, in the Bible we read of Moses who was a born leader. But he was also a tough man who took strong action when he witnessed injustice committed upon the weak or disadvantaged. It was his default setting. Moses was so wired for deliverance and justice that even when he went to a totally different place, he acted in the same way. Your question is, "Why has God made me with these tendencies and disposition?"

Answer the following Questions
1. Do you really love, respect and appreciate yourself in spite of your faults and deficiencies?
2. To what extent do you compare yourself with others? Is there anyone

whom you would rather be or whom you would rather be like instead of yourself; if so who and why?

Do the following exercises:

1. Look at yourself in the mirror every day this week and say to yourself, "I am fearfully and wonderfully made. Lord, show me what my assignment in the earth is, and cause me to fulfill some of it today."

You may repeat this exercise as often as it seems fitting to do so. You will benefit from its long-term impact.

2. Lay hands on yourself every day for seven days and say "In the name of Jesus, I deliver myself from every negative word spoken over my life by me and by others. I am royalty of God, therefore I will love and respect myself and I will show fort the

excellence of God in my life moving forward."

Make a habit out of laying your hands on your head and making declarations over your life. You will find that this liberating. It will build your confidence. More importantly, it will actually be your active part in breaking ties with the curses and covenants that you inherited from your ancestors and family tree without knowing anything about them.

Say "In the name of Jesus, I renounce every covenant made by my parents six hundred generations back. I shall live and not die. I shall reap the blessing of my ancestors who did right in the eyes of the Lord. I am an heir of the Mercies of God; and therefore I shall not pay for the evils of my ancestors."

Add to this prayer and declaration whatever you see fit; and make it a regular declaration over your own life as you lay hands upon yourself.

Attribute #13
Love others

A model Christian loves others.

I learnt a song many years ago that goes like this "God's love is like a circle, a circle big and round. And when you see a circle, no ending can be found. And so the love of Jesus goes on eternally. Forever and forever, I know that God loves me."

Love of others is not pity; it is not just empathy, and it is not mere respect. This means that you may respect people but you do not have affection for them. When I say I love you, I should mean that: a) I wish you well, b) I have good will towards, c) It is my desire that things go well for you.

1 Corinthians 13 is commonly referred to as 'the love chapter of the Bible.' Every believer should become familiar with this definition of love. The most arresting thing

about this passage is that it states emphatically that "Love never ends." This means that even if the person you love has wounded you to the point that you cannot maintain a relationship with that person, you could still wish them well.

In one church where I served as Pastor, I had a member who had to leave an abusive relationship. A few years after the legal separation, her husband was having difficulties in his life. He reached out to his former wife for help and she gave it. Her co-workers were baffled by her kindness because they knew of the torture he put her through when they were married.

Sometimes people get a divorce and then become good friends. Others often ask "How could this be?" perhaps the best answer is that people may be incompatible as husband and wife, but they can still love each other, for love never ends.

Luke 6:31 instructs us to "Do unto others as we would have them do to us."

This principle is called the golden rule. It guarantees that if people live by this rule, life will be better. Charity and graciousness will be felt all around us whenever people act with the consciousness of the needs of each other. In other words, if each of us acted with awareness and deliberate care about the needs and concerns of each other, we will be always competing in love rather than in envy, jealousy and coldness.

Rom 12:9 tells us that "Love must be sincere." The amazing thing is that if you genuinely love someone they will know it. This makes it possible for a person to be really upset with another person and still be decent about it.

One of the many stories I've heard about the Queen of Sheba when she visited King Solomon is this one: The queen brought two bouquets of flowers to the King and asked him to show his wisdom by telling her which one is real and which one is artificial. The king thought for a while and then he summoned one of his subjects. He instructed the subject to bring in a small hive of bees and let them go in a container with the flowers. As you can guess, the bees flocked to the real flowers.

You see, genuine love attracts genuine people. In 1Peter 4:8 we read, "Love each other deeply because love covers a multitude of sin." This is perhaps why people can get hurt so deeply and still relate to the one who hurt them, without trying to get back at the person, or without letting that person always feel bad continually.

      Loving others mean that we must take them seriously because you are listening to what they are really saying.

 I once had a conversation with a woman who had been out of a job for a while. She had doctorate and she was an experienced educator. She shared her story with me. She informed me that she told her associates in high places that she was broke and she needed a job. They kept making light of it because they could not think that the chips were down for her like that. I was blessed with enough money in my pocket to give her some money for gas. She was deeply appreciative.

Loving others means that we take them seriously enough to probe what they are saying to us. By doing so, we can see what that person really needs from us. We can also hear the voice of God telling us how we can possibly be His hand to the other person for their good.

Answer the following Questions

1. Do you find it hard to love others as much as you love yourself; If so why?
2. Is there anyone in your life that you just cannot bring yourself to have affection for? Do you find it hard to love that person with the love of God in spite of your inability to feel affection towards them?

Do the following exercises:

1. Over the next seventy days, make a concerted effort to tell someone everyday of these seventy days one of the following statements of assurance:

a) "You are special to God, and he had something special for you to do."

b) "You are fearfully and wonderfully made, don't take it for granted."

c) "God loves you, I love you, and your life means something to me."

2. Every day for the next seven days, Pray to God for the person whom you find it hard to love. Ask the Lord to change your attitude towards that person. Ask the Lord to change the person into being a more lovable person. Ask the Lord to reveal to you why you are unable to love the person. *[The answer to this last question may take a while].* After you get the revelation, be at peace with yourself.

Attribute #14
Know who you are!

A model Christian knows what it is to be a model Christian.

Romans 8:16 assures the believer that "God spirit bears witness with our spirit that we are children of God." When you are a believer you do know that you are saved. You do not have to second guess whether you are a child of God. Perhaps you, like me, may remember the time when you just got saved. You were not sure because you wanted to *feel* saved. Apart from that early period in your walk with God, you should not be depending on *feelings* to assure you of salvation. When you are saved, you develop the desires of a believer, the ways of a believer, and you make every effort to please God. When you are saved, you know it because it registers in your spirit.

John tells us in 1 John 5:30 "These things I have written to you that you may know..." Knowing provides you with the ability to defend your faith and to bear witness to your faith through your testimony. In like manner, a model Christian knows that he/she is a model Christian.
2 Tim 2:15 gives the believer this instruction 'Study to show yourself approved to God..." another version of the Bible says, "Work hard so God can say to you, 'well done...'

You cannot be a model Christian and be lazy at the same time. You cannot be a model Christian and be constantly complaining. You may not like what you do, but you will do it with grace and integrity anyway. I remember an experience from one church where I served as their Pastor. There was a retired man in that church who would often say to me that he is particularly moved by these words in a book of prayers, "Lord help all those who do not like the work they do..." That brother understood from his own experience, that sometimes people function under pressure and inconvenience, but if they can have the right attitude, they can still be a good witness to the glory of God.

A model Christian knows what God requires. They know this through study. He also knows the qualities that make him a model believer.

2 Timothy 3:17 tells us that 'all scripture is given by God ... to equip the believer for good work.' You cannot be a model Christian if you do not give yourself to study. It is through study that you will know how to relate even to the people who do not like you. The man or woman of God will do good to others even when that man does not feel that his goodness is fully appreciated.

In 2 chronicles 1:7 and following, we are shown that a model Christian asks God for wisdom and seeks to please God in things great and small. As a model Christian lives in the wisdom of God, he will allow God to direct and guide him in all that he needs to do.

If you are a model Christian there are certain things that you will know for sure. You will know that the unworthy things you used to do, they no longer have a place in your heart or in your desires. You know that you have desires for the things of God. You know whether you treated your loved ones poorly or graciously. You know if you harbor jealousy and envy in your heart. As a model Christian you will make yourself feel happy for the other person's progress. As a model Christian, you will help where you can because you will be assured that you are doing the will of God even though you may not get anything out of it at the moment. The model Christian knows whether he desires God with his whole heart. He knows that he genuinely wants to be good and holy. He knows that he knows whether he desires to live in the presence of God through prayers.

Being a model Christian means that you will at times experience challenges. However, you also know that you will not be destroyed. This is the reason why churches need model Christians. They are the ones who will stay around and fight on and build the church because they are available to be used by God.

A model Christian makes people in general and other believers in particular want to be like them. When people find model Christians, they know that they have found the real deal.

A model Christian wants revelation knowledge from God. It cannot be emphasized enough that you cannot become a model Christian unless you really *LISTEN* to God.

Here are five things in summary that you will know as a model Christian:

1. That the bad or destructive things you use to do, you choose not to do them anymore.

2. That you desire to receive direct revelations from God even in your dreams. That is to say, you will desire to hear from God audibly and to see signs visibly.
3. That you are a person who prays fervently and frequently. In the Bible we are told that Daniel prayed to God so often that when he was thrown into the Lion's den for doing so, the lions could not hurt him. In another story we are told of the prophet Elijah who prayed to God and caused the rain to hold up. Then he prayed to God for rain and rain fell.
4. That you are working to improve your academic knowledge about spiritual matters. It is important to go to some kind of program that teaches the Bible and teaches the applications of the biblical principles through a structured curriculum.

5. That you must listen to God. We learn from the Bible that God was showing some things to the Hebrews through Moses, yet they did not receive it. Sometimes God will give us an idea, or a revelation, but the application and manifestation of it may be for a later time. However, we will only understand the timing of the revelation by listening to God.

In the same saga of the Hebrews, we also observe that although God took the people out of Egypt, they did not let God take Egypt out of them. The point here is that a whole generation of the Hebrews did not make it into the Land of promise that God had reserved for them because they were not listening to God.

In Romans10:17 we learn that "Faith come by hearing the word of God." This is such an important principle because it highlights the importance of listening. Sometime we may see things, but our perception may be merely that – a perception. It may even be an illusion. Hence we must develop a listening ear so that we can grow in faith by what we hear rather than what we see.

Answer the following Questions
1. How close are you to being a model Christian?
2. How often do you examine your life to see whether you are actively progressing towards being a model Christian?

Do the following exercises:
1. For the next thirty days, ask God to show you who you are in the spirit realm. Ask God to tell you what kind of animal he would liken you to. For example, a psychotherapist may compare patient's personality to an Otter. That means that the person loves to be busy enjoying life. You may be a Lion or Golden Retriever etc. Pray

for a prolonged period for the Lord to improve and extend the spiritual gift that he has given you. Note that one of the main ways to enhance your spiritual gift is by practicing it.

2. Start a silent campaign to help someone you have a close relationship with, to know who they are in Christ. Work with them through the same series of exercises that you went through. This is important because it is how you will actually develop your own gifts. It is similar to how a teacher becomes more proficient in his subject area through imparting the knowledge to his student.

Attribute number #15
Sold Out

A model Christian is sold out to and for Jesus Christ. Christ is his/her all.

Remember that attributes are qualities. They are trophies of God's grace in your life. We should work hard to represent heaven, God and the idea of an angel; so that we cause others to want to be like us. It does not mean that you are a pushover. In fact we can make people unhappy and uncomfortable for God's sake. The goal is not to make people unhappy. However, we sometimes have to make people unhappy temporarily in order to secure the eventual good. So too God will let us learn some important lessons and develop some important values as believers.

My wife and I once took our sons to a street fare. They saw balloons for sale and wanted one. We told them that it may be better to wait. One of them said, "I will wait". The other son said, "No, I want the balloon." Further up the road, the one who waited got a whistle that he was happier with. Then the one, who chose not to wait, was obviously sadden because he knew that if he had waited, he would have gotten something better.

God sometimes let us wait because he has a better idea. One woman told her story of how committed she was to a man who was a violent prowess. She followed the man even to another state. She then got saved. It was then that she learnt that she had a spirit of lust and an unhealthy attachment to the man in her life. She realized that she was sold out to that man even to her own endangerment. We must become sold out to the Lord like that woman was to the man in her life that she was not even married to.

I read somewhere that the great evangelist and Church planter John Wesley, at 83yrs old was travelling around England preaching the gospel.

No matter how old or young we are, we can be sold out to the Lord.

When the spirit of the Lord is upon you, you will give yourself to the work of the Lord unreservedly.

Give yourself to the Lord, and give yourself for the Lord.

When you are fired up for the Lord, you cannot wait to get to Bible study and Church. You understand that there is no obeah man, no hymn, no candle, no communion, no saint or anything else that can give you the life and the power and the breakthrough that you need. You must get on your knees before God. When no one is watching you and you are alone even in the middle of the night, you can cry out to God and get close to Him.

In the gospel of Luke 19:1-10 we find a man called Zacchaeus. He was rich but he was miserable. Jesus had to rescue him from his misery. Having a lot of money is not a guarantee for happiness.

There was a woman who anointed Jesus feet with ointment. Jesus' disciples were not happy about this because of the reputation of the woman. When they pressed the issue, Jesus made them leave her alone because he knew that she knew where she was coming from and what he had done for her. In Philippians 3:8 the apostle Paul list the items of his pedigree. But he said that he "Count it all as dung because of the grace of God's salvation in his life." When you become sold out to God, all that you have become tools in the hands of God. Sometimes the sold out of God will receive special and unusual instructions from God. The instructions to them may be strange, but because they are sold out to God, they will go that extra mile to please God because they are sold out.

God can send you on a special assignment; and God can touch your heart and move you when you are sold out to Christ. In Matt 26:39, Jesus the supreme model for our lives said to his father "If it be possible, let this cup pass from me; nevertheless not my will but yours be done." When you are sold out for God, you will do whatever God's will is even if you would rather go in a different direction.

Paul said that he had a lot of credentials but when he encountered Christ he counted it all dung for the surpassing goodness of the glory of God.
When you are sold out for God, you never know what the Lord will do to favor you.

Jesus shows us that when we are sold out for God we will get to the point that we can even say that "The Lord has put something in my heart to do. And even if I do not feel like doing it, I will do it for the glory of God."

Some people spend too much of their time running away from God and running from their ministry. They need to surrender so that God can give them the joy that comes from surrendering to their calling. Many believers continue to live below their potential and below their real selves, because they are not sold out to the Lord.

One song says, "Something happened in my soul and now I know he touched me and made me whole." This song reflects the joy of being sold out to God. *The **knowing*** keeps us sensitive to the touch of God's hand. It makes us sensitive to the activities of God's grace. And it makes us willing to have God show us the way so that we may walk with him.

Answer the following Questions
1. Are you sold out for Christ? If so, what are the convincing marks that this is the case?
2. Are you passionate about other Christians being sold out for Christ? If so, what are you doing to make this a reality?

Do the following exercises:
1. Make a list of the changes that have taken place in your life over the past six months that can clearly show that you have grown in Christ as a believer.
2. Decide on a day and time of the week when you will lessen your activities and make time to be alone with God, to really listen to Him. This time must not be the same as the time that you use to prepare a Bible study or a lesson to be shared with others. It must not be a time that is set aside by an organization such as a church group. It must be *your personal time* that you set as an appointment with the Lord. Designate a notebook that you will use as a journal to write down the insights, the principles and the assignments that the Lord will give you during this listening period.

Reviews

****

The depth and principles presented in this book are both taught and lives by my friend pastor Dillon Burgin. This book will bless your life and take you to the next level of your spiritual walk.

Vincent A. Morgan, pastor of Lifeline Gospel Ministries Intl. New York.

****

Pastor Burgin is a teacher who has the ability to stimulate culture. He stimulates and motivates learning skills in his students. As a pastor, he is fully equipped and he is passionate about the word of God. This book is a must read for every believer who has been looking for some strategic, practical and clearly outlined directions on how to develop a model walk with God.

La Verne A. Thompson, Executive Director, Managed Health Care Trust Fund; New
****

****

Pastor Burgin is a man that's deep in the word of God both spiritually and socially. He provides great information through scholarship, teaching and administration. He labors tireless to empower our local community and beyond. This book is another tool to help in the fulfillment of that mission.

Bishop Mervin Harding, Entrepreneur & senior pastor of Grace Deliverance Tabernacle; New York.

****

I've always said that Pastor Burgin is an inspirational preacher-teacher. He is solid in the word. This book is healthy food for the spirit of all who read it. We need more men like Pastor Burgin whom God will raise up to faithfully teach and empower believers.

Roger Weller, senior pastor of Faith Evangelistic Ministries; New York.

****

****

Pastor Burgin is passionate about helping people to become all that God wants them to be. He is a visionary who knows the time, from God's perspective; and he is willing and committed to both the development and the training of others. Read this book which represents the depth of what its author offers, and watch yourself turn into a rose.

Canon Maurice Powell, celebrated Music Director & ministry consultant; New York.

****

About the Author

Pastor Dillon Burgin is the founding pastor and chief servant of *Harmony Tabernacle* in Brooklyn, New York. He is also the founder and director of '*The Rising Stars Outreach Center*' which serves the inner city, where he regularly distributes food and basic need items. Pastor Burgin loves the lord and is passionate about preaching and outreach ministry.

He has authored several books including his *"The Power and Freedom of Purpose"* which is an excellent work book that guides people to discover and function in their purpose. He is an avid playwright, as well as a passionate actor and a producer.

Pastor Burgin is the host of the popular radio show "Lens on the Logos."He also hosts a television show by the same name on New York cable television. Pastor Burgin has received awards from several organizations for his work in the wider community. He has also received proclamations from New York City officials.

You can find more information on his website at: www.pastorburgin.com

Twitter.com/dpastorburgin

Made in the USA
Charleston, SC
08 May 2016